The Angels of The Law of Attraction

Manifest Your Dreams with Divine Power

Rose Manning

CONTENTS

Ask an Angel

Every time you get The Law of Attraction to work, it's because you caught the attention of an angel. This is why it works like a miracle.

Some of the time.

This is also why it fails.

A famous Law of Attraction book once said that you should *Ask and It Is Given,* but the authors never told you who to ask. Now you know. You ask the angels, and this book will show you how.

The Law of Attraction is real, but it describes a tiny fragment of the manifestation process. Manifestation happens when you align your will with the power of the angels.

Nobody has ever shown you how to use angels to get The Law of Attraction to work, and as a result The Law of Attraction only works some of the time. The rudimentary methods shown in the most popular books can work, but there is a faster, better and more certain way of getting what you want. The answer is the angels.

The exhilarating truth is that the angels don't decide whether your wish is worthy of their attention. If you ask in the right way, it is the angels' sacred responsibility to respond to your request and give you what you ask for.

Without angels, there is no Law of Attraction. It would be lovely if you could imagine your future and have it come true, without any more effort than that. It would be wonderful if changing your thoughts changed your reality, but you can think all the positive thoughts you want and most of the time nothing is going to happen.

The good news is that you can contact angels easily. You can get them to listen and help. This works whatever your beliefs and whatever your religion. It even works if you don't believe in angels. When you act as though the angels are real, and make contact with them, you begin to manifest your dreams almost instantly.

Since this book was first published, in 2015, I have heard many wonderful stories from readers. Some people didn't like the book, but when people actually used the ideas, without judgment, the results were nothing short of astounding. As one reader put it, you should do yourself a favor and contacts these powerful and generous angels. I hope that you do.

Why The Secret Usually Doesn't Work

If you want a summary of The Law of Attraction, there are thousands of books, movies, seminars and audio recordings that all cover the same bases.

In short, you are meant to align yourself with positive thoughts and feelings and then picture the future you want. You let that future come into your life without resistance.

Sounds easy, and if all you want is a few extra dollars or a bit of extra luck, it works moderately well, for a while. If you want something more impressive, you need to make direct contact with angels.

The Law of Attraction works sometimes because, without even realizing it, you caught the attention of an angel. To manifest your desires deliberately, all you need to know is how to catch the attention of an angel, and I can teach you that in just a few minutes.

To get this method to work every time, you need to know why the Law of Attraction fails so often. Only when you know that, can I reveal the methods for making angelic contact safely and peacefully.

As I see it, there are five keys to The Law of Attraction. You could summarize it in one paragraph, or twenty-five principles, or thirty-seven books, but it all boils down to these five concepts.

Every one of these is a great idea, but without The Angels of The Law of Attraction, these principles don't always work.

You're about to find out why.

Manifestation Principle One

Find out what you really want, so that you can go with the flow.

If you spend lots of time visualizing a future that you don't sincerely want, you're fighting yourself and doing battle with your soul. You might be picturing a new job and sending lots of good feelings at that new job, but really, if you're honest with yourself, all you want is a six-month holiday. Knowing what you want is vital for manifestation, but sadly, most people can't get this one right.

The Problem

Without angelic guidance, it's almost impossible to know what you really want. You may *think* you want more money, but what you *really* want is more relief from the pressure of work. You may *think* you want a different job, but *really* you want more money. You may *think* you want to win the lottery, but *really* you want a life of mystery and adventure. Even when you've spent years pursuing a dream, you may find out it's not what you want at all, which is why it's never come to you.

The Solution

When you work with angels, they can help guide you to get a clear vision of what you really want. This might not be what you think you *should* want. It might not be what your parents or partner *expect* of you. This will be what *you* really want. The angels can guide you to find your true desires. This single power kicks The Law of Attraction into action.

Manifestation Principle Two

You create with every thought, so imagine that your dream has come true.

Many people believe that we create our reality with every thought. If you spend enough time picturing your reality, that reality can come into being.

The Problem

Our thoughts *can* create reality, it's true. Our thoughts are passed on to the angels, and reality falls into place just as we desire. The major problem here is that Law of Attraction gurus have taken this observation and turned it into a rule that says *every thought you have, changes your world, every time, so everything is **your fault***. If The Law of Attraction doesn't work for you, they say, then there's something wrong with your thoughts. This is not true and trying to control or limit your thoughts to ensure manifestation is difficult, impractical and ineffective.

The second part of the problem is that there's no real agreement on how you are meant to visualize. Some authors say you only need to visualize for seventeen seconds, and others say you need to stare at Vision Boards (covered with pictures of things you want in your life) to make it work. Others change their mind about what you're meant to do each time a new book comes out. Visualization is meant to be the key to all this, but it's never explained well or made workable.

The Solution

In the real world, you can think whatever thoughts you want and still attract an amazing future. If you know what you want, the angels will carry your desire until it manifests in reality.

Manifestation Principle Three

Let go of resistance.

It's assumed that when you have a desire, you must be resisting it in some way; otherwise it would have manifested by now. When you try to manifest something, you must let go of your desire for it to manifest.

The Problem

When you want something, you're supposed to stop wanting it until it appears. Some people even try to forget about the very thing they are trying to manifest. Although there are good reasons for this principle, the way it's usually taught leaves you uncertain about when you're meant to be thinking positive thoughts and when you're meant to forget about your desire. Many people find it impossible to find a balance between using their thoughts to manifest, and emptying their mind of all desire. Letting go of resistance becomes a frustrating part of the process.

The Solution

You hand your desire over to the angels, which makes it easy to let go of resistance. By giving your request to the angels, you automatically relax and know that the result will come. When you remember the result you want or desire it strongly, nothing goes wrong, because it's all in the hands of an angel.

Manifestation Principle Four

Feel grateful for the result when it comes.

Gratitude is undoubtedly an important part of the manifestation process. When you enjoy your manifestations, you get more of them.

The Problem

If your Grandpa gives you a delicious dinner, you don't feel generally grateful to God and The Universe; you feel grateful *to* your Grandpa. But when it comes to The Law of Attraction, who are you meant to be grateful to? You might find yourself trying to be grateful, but you're not sure where to send those feelings.

The Solution

When you ask the angels for help, you know who to thank. You know the angels have done their work, and you automatically feel gratitude toward them. This makes the process almost automatic.

Manifestation Principle Five

Feel grateful in general.

If you're the sort of person who enjoys a cool breeze as much as you enjoy a windfall of cash (and if you're able to feel grateful for these pleasures), then more pleasure will come your way.

The Problem

Positive thinking is overrated. To be fully human we need to experience the full spectrum of emotions. To wallow in misery is no fun, but to pretend you're happy all the time is to deny the rich complexity of life that is on offer. Most approaches to The Law of Attraction insist that you get rid of all negative thoughts, and focus only on the positive so that you can send out gratitude all the time. It's just too hard, and when you go to a funeral or see your pet die, or lose your job, it feels fake pretending it's all Meant To Be. You want to recover to a place of gratitude – of course you do – but you should be able to experience the real emotions you feel, without worrying that all your manifestation work will come undone.

The Solution

Trust that the angels will help you to feel the full spectrum of emotions, and will not punish you for feeling bad. They can also help you to appreciate the smaller moments of joy, so that it is easy to feel gratitude for simple, everyday pleasures. Contact with the angels can give you an authentic way to feel gratitude.

A Need and a Name

Ok, you're convinced! You like the idea of The Law of Attraction, and you want to get going. How do you get started?

The wonderful thing is that you won't have to spend hours making vision boards, or writing down affirmations or creating thought vibrations or imagining your way into a new reality. All that's required is a need and a name.

Your need is easy to get hold of. You're probably aware of what you need, right now. In any given moment, you probably have many needs. Your need does not have to be virtuous. You are not trying to impress the angels with your holiness. If you need more money - because you're going to be happier with some extra cash in the bank - that's your genuine need. Be honest!

You also need the name of an angel. In fact, to get this process to work, you will send your request up through the ranks of angels. By doing this, your request will be acknowledged by several great archangels.

There are books out there that suggest you should contact one angel for travel, another for earning money, and a different set of angels entirely if you want to find love. These complex theories are interesting, and I hear they can work, but since ancient times it has been known that there is an order of archangels that can unlock the magic of manifestation.

These are the angels you will contact:

Gabriel

Raphael

Haniel

Michael

Camael

Raziel

Metatron

You may be familiar with some of these names, but others may be new to you. If you research these angels, you will find lots of information, and some of it is extreme and outrageous, while some is quite accurate. If you do much reading, you'll find that there are lots of contradictions. People have been writing about angels for thousands of years, and to make things worse, people have been writing about them on the internet in recent years, making all sorts of wild guesses.

My advice is to limit your research. I'm not saying you should avoid all information, but that information is never consistent, and it won't help your work. It's far better to *try* this angelic attraction process and see that it works. You will probably find out more about these angels by working with them than you could ever discover by reading books. That's why I'm keeping this book short. To get manifesting you have to start communicating with the angels, so I'll get out of your way and let can do that.

How do you make contact? If you have a strong need and the name of the angel, *that is all you need*. The exact process is explained in the following chapter. If you think this all sounds a bit complicated, because you just want to visualize your future and have The Law of Attraction drop something in your lap, don't worry. The process of contacting the angels takes only seconds once you've learned the basics, and that should only take you a very short time.

The Seven Angels of Manifestation

You can contact the angels any time you like, whether you're walking down the street, climbing a mountain or falling asleep in bed. When you're starting out, it's best to find somewhere quiet to sit, so that you can concentrate on what you're doing.

Think about what it is that you want to manifest. You may want something small; to find a lost object, to heal a friendship, or to win some money. You may want something much greater, such as a change of career, to buy a new home or to win an award. The process is the same whatever the size of your problem.

When you think about what it is that you want to manifest, you will notice the lack of it.

In this moment, if you want to find a lost object, it's because the object is lost – you lack it. When you contact the angels, you change your feelings from one of loss and lack, to a feeling of having. Here's how it works.

Let's imagine that you've applied for a new job, and you really want to get that job. First, you contact Gabriel. You are not praying to this angel, and you are not pleading for help. Angels are messengers, ready to hear your request. By contacting these angels, you are sending your message to the top, where your request will be heard. As you make your request, your feeling will change from one of lack to one of relief. This is the magic of angelic contact.

You can speak out loud, or think of the words in your head. You can do this in whatever way you like, but you should remember that you are contacting great archangels. Although you do not have to grovel, it is wise to know that you are contacting mighty angels, and that the simple act of trying to contact the angel guarantees that contact is made.

Think, or say, something like, 'Angel Gabriel, I would like to get the job that I applied for.'

It can be as simple as that. There's no need to ask for a job interview, or ask that you perform well at the interview, or ask to be seen in a good light – just ask for the *final result* that you want to manifest. The angels will know what you mean, and what steps are required to get you there.

Gabriel is an angel of promise, so feel relief that your request has been heard.

Pause for a few moments to really feel that relief, and then you contact Raphael. There's no need to change the wording. You're making the same request to a different angel, so that you can say (or think), 'Angel Raphael, I would like to get the job that I applied for.'

Know that Raphael is an angel who can heal a situation, so feel relief at the healing that Raphael can bring. (Remember, this isn't necessarily healing an illness, but healing a situation. If you want a new job, it's because you don't have the job. Raphael can help heal that situation by getting you the job you want.) Really let yourself feel that sense of healing.

The third angel is Haniel. Repeat your request to Haniel. If you find that the wording changes slightly, that's OK. This often happens, and it's absolutely normal. You're not chanting holy words; you're just asking an angel for something that you want. You can also keep the phrase exactly the same, if that's easier.

Haniel is an angel of harmony, so feel relief that Haniel will bring harmony into your life, by granting your request.

The fourth angel is Michael. Make your request to Michael, just as you have done before, and know that Michael is an angel of general welfare. Feel relief that Michael can improve your welfare by granting your wish.

The fifth angel is Camael. Make your request to Camael, just as you have before. Camael is an angel of strength, so feel relief that you will gain strength from having your wish granted.

The sixth angel is Raziel who knows all the secrets of reality. Make your request to Raziel, and feel relief that Raziel knows the secret to making your wish come true.

The seventh and final angel is Metatron, who is an angel of infinity. Make your request to Metatron, and feel relief that all your dreams will come true.

This might sound like a long process, but once you get used to it, it takes nothing more than a couple of minutes. It's certainly a lot faster than doing lengthy visualizations, spending hours trying to control your thoughts.

You'll notice that after you speak your request, you are told to feel relief. This is important. This is your gift of trust to the angels. When you feel relief, you are showing the angels that you have faith in the result. Feel the relief as you contact the angel, as though you *know* the angel has now taken over your problem and will bring you the result you want. This paragraph is possibly the most important in the entire book, so don't neglect this part of your communication.

How often do you make your request? That's up to you. Some people make the request just once, and then let go and let the result come about when it comes about. Others prefer to ask every day until the desire manifests as a result. My advice is to ask once, and if you were able to feel complete relief, and if you believe that it really is in the hands of the angels, then you can stop. If you still feel some doubt or concern, perform this process every day until you feel that the angels have heard your call, or until the result manifests.

You can make twenty different requests a day, for small and large things, but make each request separately. Don't say, 'Gabriel, I ask that you find my lost cat, bring me some money and help me get fit.' Instead, perform the entire process for one request, then let some time go by, and make your next request.

Don't chase your results. When you have spoken to Metatron – out loud or in your thoughts – know that you have handed your desire over to the angels. It is now your task to trust that the angels will do their work. If you keep looking for your result or wondering why it hasn't manifested yet, you are sending a message to the angels that you don't trust them. If your desired wish bubbles up in your mind, remember the relief the angels bring and focus on that relief, rather than on your desire.

At the same time, you need to help the angels out. Although you've handed the problem over to them, this doesn't mean that you should now avoid your life. If you've asked to get a new job, it's your responsibility to prepare well for the job interview in every possible way. When you do, the angels will help.

If you've asked for more money, it's your job to keep your eyes out for new opportunities, or even just hints of intuition that can guide you to more money. When you do that, the angels will help.

If you've asked to find love, do not sit at home waiting for your soulmate. Get out and meet as many people as you can, warmly and without expectation. When you do that, the angels will help.

Know, too, that if you request something small, it's more likely to manifest rapidly than if you request a huge life change. This isn't always the case, but it's often true, so if you ask for a massive change, don't worry if it takes time to manifest. Time is your friend and makes the change easier to cope with. Know that the angels are using that time to set up that best situation for you.

Remember, you are not praying or begging for help. You are asking for something that you feel is in line with your purpose in life. The angels will respond.

The Process Summarized

Use this summary only when you have read the previous chapter in full.

Make your request to Gabriel, and feel relief that your request has been heard.

Make your request to Raphael and feel relief at the healing that Raphael can bring.

Make your request to Haniel and feel relief that Haniel will bring harmony into your life, by granting your request.

Make your request to Michael and feel relief that Michael can improve your welfare by granting your wish.

Make your request to Camael, and feel relief that you will gain strength from having your wish granted.

Make your request to Raziel, and feel relief that Raziel knows the secret to making your wish come true.

Make your request to Metatron, and feel relief that all your dreams will come true.

Trust that the angels are doing the work for you. Patience and trust will bring more results than doubt and eagerness.

Angelic Manifestation

Let's revisit the manifestation principles of The Law of Attraction and see how they apply now.

Find out what you really want so that you can go with the flow.

When you start manifesting with the angels, you will find that you begin to change. You will understand your desires more clearly. You may gain intuition into what you really want. As soon as you make contact with these angels, they will guide you on the path that is most likely to bring you happiness and fulfillment.

You create with every thought, so imagine that your dream has come true.

For you, there's no need to imagine anything. You've handed your desire to the angels, so let them work miracles in your life. Your thought is a creative force, but it has been handed to the angels as a request, and there is no need to keep thinking positive thoughts.

Let go of resistance.

Every time you contact the angels, you feel relief, so there is no need to focus on resistance. Know that your wish is in the hands of the angels and you'll be utterly free of all resistance.

Feel grateful for the result when it comes.

You asked the angels, so when your result comes about, you will automatically remember the angels, and you will feel gratitude. It couldn't be easier.

Feel grateful in general.

When you work with angels, you will begin to enjoy the simplest pleasures as well as seeing the greatness that awaits you. This happens without effort.

Does it Matter How You Say The Names?

Most of the time, you'll be doing this work silently, simply thinking the names, but you might still want to get the pronunciation right. If you're saying your request out loud – as some people prefer to do – you'll feel better if you're saying these names correctly.

The great news is that the angels don't need you to pronounce their names perfectly. They understand your need, they understand that you have seen an English version of an ancient name, and they understand that you're doing your best to pronounce it correctly. That is always good enough.

To make it easier, though, these are the most common pronunciations for these angelic names.

Gabriel

Gabriel is often pronounced gay-bree-ell. Another common pronunciation is gabb-ree-ell. Some even say gah-bree-ell.

Raphael

Raphael is usually pronounced raff-eye-ell, but some people also say raff-ah-ell.

Haniel

Many people pronounce Haniel with a silent H, so that it sounds like are-nee-ell. Others prefer har-nee-ell, or a softer hah-nee-ell.

Michael

Most people say this just like the common name Michael, although some put in a bit more emphasis to make it mike-ell or mike-ull. You also hear this pronounced as meek-ah-ell, which is quite close to the Hebrew pronunciation.

Camael

You can say this angel's name as cam-ee-ell or cam-ah-ell.

Raziel

The great angel Raziel can be addressed as raz-ee-ell or rah-zee-ell.

Metatron

This is probably the most straightforward name, with most people pronouncing it just as you'd guess - met-a-tron. Occasionally you will hear met-ah-tron or met-ah-trawn.

You have all the knowledge you need to manifest your desires, so get started.

How Do I Know All This?

If you're wondering how I know all this, you can probably guess the answer. The angels told me. I'm one of those people you hear about who had a close call with death, and in the aftermath, I had a brush with the angels. I didn't see heaven, and I don't know why I was chosen to live on beyond the accident, but in those few moments of divine contact, I was shown how angels work with The Law of Attraction. Ever since that day I have known that it is part of my purpose to share the knowledge that the angels shared with me. I am doing that with this book.

This is a short and simple book, but one that I care about a great deal. At this point, you can assume I'm crazy, or you can give the process a try. The only way to find out if it works is to *try* this process. Please try this out, following the instructions exactly. Start with something small but significant, and you will be pleasantly surprised.

I believe that this is the way The Law of Attraction works. If I'm wrong, you have nothing to lose but a few minutes of your time, and then you can get a refund on the book, write a horrible review and make me look like an insane woman who believes the angels spoke to her.

If I'm **right**, then manifest the life you want and let the world know: *this is how The Law of Attraction works.* When you join in with the power of the angels, the angels will reward you.

Rose Manning

Made in the USA
Columbia, SC
16 November 2020